EARLY LOS ANGELES

By Harry Knill
& the best old authorities

"Los Angeles has a history, sir. It always was an important place, sir."

Lower, or Old, California was discovered by Jiménez, one of Cortez's captains, in 1533, but not until 1697 was it settled by Padre Salvatierra and the Jesuits. Seventy years later the Jesuits, in thanks for their years of toil, were expelled. Franciscan friars were soon assigned to take their places. Then, in 1769, those friars were sent north into Upper, or New, California to convert the natives to Christianity and make them into good subjects of His Catholic Majesty, King Carlos III of Spain. Led by Padre Junípero Serra, they established missions from the Bay of San Diego to the Bay of San Francisco.

The "Sacred Expedition" by both land and sea was directed by José de Gálvez, the king's Visitor General to New Spain. Captain Fernando Rivera y Moncada (below, I think) led the land troop up from Loreto, the capital of both Californias. It was Captain Rivera who would recruit, with difficulty, the first settlers for the *Pueblo* or Town of *La Reyna de los Angeles*—The Queen of the Angels. In that first year of the Spanish conquest, 1769, missions and *presidios*, or forts, were established at San Diego and at Monterey. The founding of Mission San Gabriel Arcángel was decided upon the next year; it was that mission which would soon have the pueblo of other angels as a neighbor. Padre Serra and Captain Fages, the commandant, decided the mission should be near the *Río de Nombre de Jesus de los Temblores*—Earthquake River, named by Captain Portolá in 1769, for the earth trembled violently when he was there. It was afterwards known as the Río de Santa Ana. Since Padre Serra was at

CAPTAIN FERNANDO RIVERA Y MONCADA AND A *SOLDADO DE CUERA* or leather-jacket soldier in Old California just before the expeditions to New California, by Padre Tirsch, 1767, Prague, State Library

MISIÓN DE SAN GABRIEL ARCÁNGEL DE LOS TEMBLORES by Ferdinand Deppe, 1831

". . . arrived at the mission of San Gabriel. At the mission there was one priest, fifteen soldiers, and about one thousand Indians. They had about eighty thousand head of stock, fine fields and vineyards, in fact, it was a paradise on earth." —Kit Carson, 1830

"This looks like the Promised Land," said Padre Paterna. Painting: Santa Barbara Mission Archives

The Indians, before coming to the mission, used whistles made from bones, and wooden fifes, for music. At San Gabriel, their "band of musick consists of two violins, one bass violin, a trumpet and a triangle. They made tolerable good musick."—Harrison Rogers with Jedediah Smith's party of trappers, 1826

Monterey, Captain Fages decided to found the mission without him. Padres Somera and Cambon and a corporal, ten leather-jacket soldiers from the Loreto presidio, two Catalan Volunteers from Old Spain, and six muleteers, left San Diego on August 6, 1770, for the site. After a few days' march they arrived at their destination, where they were met by a fierce horde of very angry natives. The situation was dangerous. Suddenly the fathers raised a beautiful banner on which was painted Our Lady of Sorrows, *La Dolorosa*. The warriors were overawed. They put down their arms and surrendered to "the Sovereign Queen," who became the mission's foundress.

The fathers searched for the best spot for the mission and decided upon one along what is now known as the Río Hondo, then the Río de San Miguel. It had good soil, ample water and timber, but five years later it was to become *Misión Vieja* when the fathers moved to a better location. At the founding, September 8, 1771, the birthday of the "Sovereign Queen of the Angels," a large cross was raised and blessed by Padre Cambon, who dedicated the mission and its land to God and King Carlos III. The first church was built of poles and roofed with tules. It was surrounded with a stockade.

Not until 1772 did Padre Serra himself see Mission San Gabriel. He marveled, then, at the great wide valley, perfect for founding a city. "The place was the most excellent of all discovered," he wrote. Padre Crespí, with Portolá three years before, said that it had "all the requisites for a large settlement."

A LEATHER-JACKET SOLDIER OF CALIFORNIA
by Padre Tirsch, Prague

"Their weapons are a sword, a musket, a shield, and an armor of four layers of tanned, white deerskin, which covers the entire body like a sleeveless coat; otherwise they wear what they like."—Padre Baegert

The soldiers who first came with Don Fernando forgot their leather jackets, according to Padre Serra.

On March 22, 1774, Captain Anza and his company arrived at San Gabriel on the first difficult trek overland from Sonora to Monterey. Two years later he was again at San Gabriel, on his second expedition. This time he met Captain Rivera; Rivera was on his way to San Diego because of the Indian massacre there. Anza joined Rivera and made a detour to the site of destruction. The damage done was awful. The Indians of San Gabriel, in contrast, were described by Padre Font as peaceful and of good heart. They were of medium stature, and the men went entirely naked before coming to the mission. The women wore a deerskin and cloak of otter or rabbit skin. They were attracted to the mission by their stomachs, for the land did not supply enough food, and they were too far from the sea to fish.

When the Spanish first came, the Indians rejected the food they offered and buried it secretly in the woods. Some time after, when they came to where the food had been buried, "their surprise knew no bounds when they beheld an infinity of stalks and plants unknown to them, protruding through the earth. . . A great number of their young men being hunters, they of course had their peculiar superstitions. During a hunt they never tasted food; nor on their return did they partake of what they themselves killed, from an idea that whoever ate of his own game hurt his hunting abilities," said Hugo Reid.

A *MAJORDOMO* OR RANCH FOREMAN from Old California, shortly before the founding of Los Angeles, by Padre Tirsch He is dressed as the pueblo's settlers would have been.

Modo de Pelear de los Indios de Californias, 1791, after a sketch by Tomás Suría in the *Museo Naval*, Madrid

"If an affair of this kind ever results in a defeat of our troops, it will be irreparable if the Indians come to know their power." "It is highly useful to the service of the King and the public welfare that the Indians of these establishments do not learn to kill soldiers." —Filipe de Neve, 1777, '82

"The majority of our Indians have not yet acquired much love for our way of life, for they see and meet their pagan relatives in the forest, fat and robust and enjoying liberty." —Padre Lasuén, 1797

"Their huts were made of sticks, covered in around with flag mats worked or plaited; each village contained from 500 to 1500 huts. The men wore no clothing, but the women had a deerskin wrapped round the middle." —Hugo Reid

On July 14, 1781, thirty-five soldiers led by Lieutenant González and Ensign Argüello arrived at San Gabriel. The soldiers were recruited by Captain Rivera to found the new presidio or fort of Santa Bárbara, 100 miles to the north. As agricultural products would be needed for that new presidio and for the one at San Diego—both poor spots for farming—Viceroy Croix and Governor Neve wanted Captain Rivera to recruit twenty-four farm families to settle in the rich plain near San Gabriel Mission. There they would build the second pueblo in Upper California; the first pueblo was San José on the Guadalupe River, established November 29, 1777, between the northern presidios of Monterey and San Francisco, which were also not good places for agriculture. Poor Captain Rivera looked long for twenty-four families willing to go to such a remote and desolate place, where everything was known to be outrageously costly to import. He finally found eleven families. They came across the Gulf of California to Loreto and up the peninsula and arrived at San Gabriel on August 18, 1781. These settlers or *pobladores* had agreed to stay in the new pueblo for ten years. Each family was to receive in return money and rations, two horses, two mares, two cows and a calf, two sheep, two goats, one mule, one yoke of oxen, a plow and other tools. These supplies were to be repaid from the crops which would be grown at the new settlement; there would be no taxes for five years.

A SOLDIER OF CALIFORNIA, 1791, wearing his *cuera blanca* (white leather jacket) after a sketch made by José Cardero in the *Museo Naval*, Madrid. With the Royal Regulations of 1772, the uniform of the presidio soldier was a short jacket of blue cloth with red cuffs and collar, blue breeches, a blue cloth cap, a cartridge pouch, a bandolier with the name of the presidio on it, and a black neckerchief, besides the leather jacket.

On August 26, Governor Neve issued instructions for the pueblo's founding. It was to be along the *Río de Porciúncula*, named after St. Francis' church, *Santa Maria degli Angelli*, on a *tiny portion* of land near Assisi. The river had been discovered on the second of the two days of Our Lady of the Angels of Porciúncula, August 2, 1769. The pueblo was named *La Reyna de los Angeles*, recalling also the foundress of Mission San Gabriel. The *pobladores* were put in quarantine a little distance from the mission when they arrived because some of the children had just had smallpox. On September 4, the pueblo was formally founded, now with twelve families, forty-six people: Indians, blacks, mestizos, Spanish. A plaza 200 x 200 feet was laid out with the corners facing north, east, south, and west, and three streets ran perpendicularly from each of the four sides. House lots 20 x 40 varas (55 x 110 feet) and four fields, 200 varas or 550 feet square, were given to each family, assigned by lot. Huts of mud and poles were made, along with an irrigation ditch. Better adobe houses came later. The pueblo was put under the jurisdiction of the new Santa Bárbara presidio, although San Gabriel Mission was still under the jurisdiction of San Diego. From the time of the settlement of Upper California in 1769, the padres and the military had had disputes between themselves. It wasn't clear to one side that the other's goals were important, too. Now there was a third group: the *pobladores*. And right from the beginning, a number of rascals were to be found in both

A CALIFORNIA SOLDIER'S WIFE, 1791 after Cardero; she wears an *enagua,* or transparent muslin skirt and pearls from Baja California; a tight-fitting silk blouse joins the skirt. The shoes, *zapatos de patillo,* had high wooden heels. A silk *rebozo* or shawl was also worn.

The Pueblo of Los Angeles was founded to provide supplies
for the Royal Presidios or forts of Santa Bárbara, shown here,
and San Diego. The pueblo was just between those two posts.
This view is after a sketch made in 1793 by John Sykes, who
was with Vancouver's expedition. This presidio was pronoun-
ced the best in California that year. The present rebuilding of
the old Spanish presidio in Santa Bárbara is probably the most
exciting archaeological and restoration project in California,
and it is worth the trip to see it.

the upper pueblo, San José, and the lower, Los Angeles: they were soon kicked out as useless. None of those who remained could even sign their names; that is why so little is known of the early days of the pueblo. Padre Senan wrote: "New settlers should be energetic workers, otherwise new settlements will be in danger of sharing the sad fate of the pueblos of San José de Guadalupe and Nuestra Señora de los Angeles de Porciúncula. These settlements are hardly worthy to be called towns. The main fault lies in the colonists' indifference, and their disinclination toward hard work; they prefer to hold a deck of cards rather than a hoe or plow. What little progress is made is due to the neighboring Indians and not to the settlers. The Indians cultivate the fields, do the planting, and harvest the crops; they do just about everything. I have good reason to accuse the settlers of laziness."

Sometimes the Indians did not tolerate such treatment. In 1781, the Yuma Indians, tired of seeing their fields taken over, massacred seventy-year-old Captain Rivera and his men at the new settlements on the Colorado River. In 1785 Toypurnia, a powerful and attractive twenty-four-year-old Indian woman, a wise and feared sorceress among the Gabrieleño Indians, started an uprising at San Gabriel Mission. The padres and soldiers were all to have been killed. Warriors from at least eight settlements followed Toypurnia and climbed over the walls and into the mission during the night of October 25. Toypurnia had promised that the padres would all be dead. But the soldiers had been warned. They lay in the church, dressed as dead padres awaiting burial. Suddenly, with a cry of *"Santiago!"* they rose and captured the intruders. Governor Fages came down from Monterey for the trial. Toypurnia said in court to

DANCING *EL JARABE* IN CALIFORNIA by Padre Tirsch

the governor, "I hate the padres and all of you for living here on my native soil, for trespassing upon the land of my forefathers." But soon afterwards she decided to become a Christian. In the book of baptisms for the year 1787 her name appears as Regina Josefa Toypurnia. This queen later married a Spanish soldier, and Governor Fages stood as her sponsor.

The new Angeleños did some work, irrigating and farming, and their numbers increased as retired soldiers settled in the town. By 1786, the nine families had grown to twenty-six—a population of 139. By 1791 there were 315 souls; children grew up and had families, and California families had ten children or more in those days. By 1820, there were 650 Angeleños, and in 1823, after the days of the glorious rule of Spain, there were 764. In 1790 the pueblo produced more grain than any of the missions except San Gabriel; the pueblo also had 12,000 horses and cattle that year. In 1792, unruly folk were ordered out of town—again—but they failed to go. A jail was built in 1798, and malefactors were soon escaping from it. The Angeleños "find it more necessary to gamble and play the guitar than to teach their children," still complained the mission fathers.

By 1798, five private ranchos had been granted nearby: San Rafael or La Zanja was granted in 1784 to retired Corporal José Verdugo; Los Nietos rancho was granted the same year; San Pedro was granted to J. J. Domínguez; Portezuelo was granted to the Verdugos; and Encino was granted to Francisco Reyes; his house became Mission San Fernando in 1797.

A project to build a church in town began in 1811; there had been a little chapel there, but it was now unfit, and San Gabriel was ten miles away. Construction was slow until Padre Payeras called upon the missions for help; they gave barrels of brandy to raise money, and huge quantities were consumed by the Angeleños in enthusiasm for their spiritual welfare (Bancroft's pun). The adobe building began to rise. Finally, the *brea* roof was on, and the *Nueva Iglesia de Nuestra Señora de los Angeles* was dedicated on December 8, 1822. Three bells from San Gabriel were provided; two had been made in Massachusetts. Another Yankee bell, with the best tone of all, was given by Captain Fitch as penance for having eloped with Josefa Carrillo after Governor Echeandía (who wanted her himself) had stopped them at the altar from marrying.

THROWING THE BULL BY TWISTING ITS TAIL, *colear un toro,* by Padre Tirsch

"A bull fight in California is far different from the brutal exhibitions of Spain or Mexico. Here, the bull is not killed, or lacerated; the object of the amusement being merely the exhibition of equestrian performances. The more valiant appear on foot; and as they nimbly escape danger, or boldly throw themselves into it, the interest is exceedingly increased."

In the early days of California the men did not cut their hair; it was combed and made into a long braid or tail of three strands which often came down to the waist. These tails were all cut off, with many tears, in 1822 when the government changed to the Mexican Empire. The men wore black silk handkerchiefs around their heads, under their hats, which were worn to one side "if they wished to appear dashing." Short blue or black knee pants were worn at first, with garters of gold or silver lace called *galóns.* The pants had edging up the outsides of the split legs, with five or six buttons, of which usually only one or two were buttoned. Embroidered leggings of *gemuza,* a chamois made of an entire sheep, deer or calf skin folded over, were worn, strapped on by a ribbon or silk trimmed with sequins and lace "to give a glittering effect." Short pants gave way in 1832 to *calzoneras,* long pantaloons, also split on the outside, now from hip to foot, with a row of buttons on either edge of the opening, laced together nearly down to the knee, as shown here. The *vaqueros* or cowboys still preferred short pants, as they were more convenient for their work.

The government of the early pueblo was an *ayuntamiento* or town council, with an *alcalde* or mayor (who carried a black baton with a gold knob, and beat a drum to summon the citizens), *regidores* or councilmen, and a *comisado,* who represented the governor and settled all disputes. The *comisado* was done away with after the change of government to the Republic of Mexico, which took place in Los Angeles in 1823. The introduction of republican ideas did not make the pueblo a more orderly place. Many revolutions and battles would take place there, beginning with. . .

VICTORIA'S END at the CAHUENGA PASS, 1831

Viva los Insurrectos!

Lt. Col. Don Manuel Victoria, a black man "as bold as a lion," was Military Chief of Lower California. He requested to be transferred to Upper California and succeeded after much persistence. He set out by land and finally reached Mission San Luis Rey. There he decided to reverse the policy of his predecessor, Echeandía, which had been to secularize the missions and their vast lands. The Californians would not like this, for they had their own eyes set on those great tracts of real estate. Upon reaching Monterey, Victoria, "haughty and with his head full of vanity," annulled the Secularization Decree. He then had an innocent soldier shot and a young Indian and another soldier shot for mere pilfering. Victoria kept on issuing decrees and jailing and exiling people without trials.

Some of those on Victoria's list met and asked that he call the Assembly. Victoria, "infuriated more than a snake that had been stepped on," swore revenge for this insolence and threatened to abolish the Assembly altogether. José Antonio Carrillo was among those exiled for no stated crime. (The mayor of Los Angeles, Victoria's ally Vicente Sanchez, had caused Carrillo's exile to Lower California.) From there, José Antonio planned a revolution; he rode to San Diego and met, secretly and in the dark of night, with Juan Bandini and Pío Pico (two men Victoria had intended to hang) and Abel Stearns. As soon as Victoria

COSTUMES OF THE COUNTRY by Wm. Meyers, 1842. Bancroft Library. Glazed *sombreros apilonados* or stovepipe hats are worn here, and on this page a colorful *serape;* the open *calzoneras* (pantaloons) expose the *calzoncillos* (drawers).

heard about their plan he left Monterey on the double, hoping to surprise the rebels. But the rebels had anticipated this and left for Los Angeles. Vicente Sanchez, afraid now of Carrillo, José Maria Ávila and Andrés Pico, whom he had also jailed, left town. Captain Portilla arrived with thirty San Diegans; in Los Angeles he gathered about 200 more. On December 5, 1831, he learned that Victoria was approaching with only thirty men. As Victoria neared Los Angeles, Captain Portilla occupied a strategic point on top of some hills and waited for him. Brave Captain Pacheco was with Victoria, and because of the difference in their numbers, he advised against a fight just then. Victoria answered with a remark about officers who wore women's skirts. Pacheco replied that he was man enough, and rode to the head of the troops.

Victoria reached the foot of the hill, around Cahuenga, and shouted up to Portilla to leave that bunch of rascals and join him. Portilla ordered the governor to halt, and Victoria shouted back an insult. With that, Pacheco, thinking the advance would follow, dashed toward the enemy. He met Ávila, a man of Herculean stature and perhaps the best horseman of all the inhabitants of Los Angeles, and slashed at him with his sabre. Ávila parried the slash with a pole on which he had fastened a bayonet to make a lance. As Pacheco sped past, Ávila turned and shot and killed him instantly.

Ávila did not know Victoria by sight, but when he heard Victoria shouting he realized that that man, of undistinguished figure and badly dressed with an ordinary red flannel shirt, was the chief. He made his horse jump towards Victoria, who was unable to shield his chest against Ávila's lance. Victoria fell at the same time Ávila received at point-blank a shot in his hip and fell, too. Victoria, seeing Ávila lying there, approached with the intention of finishing him off with his sword, but Ávila grasped Victoria's foot, and, pulling with great force, made him fall on his back; then Ávila reached for a knife in his boot (*bota*). Fortunately for Victoria, it was lost. A nephew of Ávila, Tomás Talamantes, noticed that the soldiers were killing his uncle. Although he was alone, he spurred his horse to defend the dying man. The first target of Talamantes' sabre was Victoria. One of the soldiers put his carbine in the way and stopped the blow; but Victoria was wounded in the face by it anyway. Talamantes, in a rain of shots, now fled, for everyone else was gone. Carrillo and Portilla, seeing that Pacheco and Ávila were dead and that Victoria comman-

José María Ávila's restored adobe house is located on Olvera Street, Los Angeles.

LOS ANGELES from the south, 1848   by Wm. Hutton, Huntington Library

ded good men, realized that the uprising was not the easy thing of words and papers: they fled like cowards, leaving the wounded Victoria victor on the field of battle. But Victoria needed confession more than further fighting. Those who flew compensated for their weak spirits by bluff, and even though they had used a great deal of this since the beginning of the uprising, they still had twice as much in reserve. They never dared explain why they did not help Talamantes and Ávila, who were the only ones among the 200 who entered combat and distinguished themselves by their courage. Portilla and Carrillo did not even admit their defeat.

Victoria, with two corpses beside him, thought that he soon might be one himself, so he left for San Gabriel Mission and sent for an English doctor. When he was out of danger of dying but still in sorry condition, he sent for Sr. Echeandía and turned the powers over to him. The Assembly was called to Los Angeles, and Victoria was sent back to Mexico on board the *Pocahontas*. But Echeandía refused to attend the Assembly, and Pío Pico was chosen by it as political chief, although Echeandía refused to accept this. Then Captain Zamorano, who did not like California or the Californians, appointed himself to this position and also to that of military chief, and he formed a party with people of the north.

Zamorano sent Lieutenant Ibarra to Los Angeles with about 100 men; Captain Barosso, with fourteen men and a cannon, met Ibarra at the San Gabriel River. Echeandía, thinking the northerners were going to take away his office, moved to Los Angeles, marching there with 200 men and six cannon. So Ibarra evacuated Los Angeles, and Echeandía entered the town, now with more than 1,000 mounted Indians and 300 soldiers. But this time, in order to avoid bloodshed, Echeandía and Zamorano arranged to divide Upper California between themselves; Zamorano took the part above Santa Bárbara, Echeandía that below. And in spite of them both, the Assembly claimed that *it* was sovereign.

Victoria had written to Mexico City that there was great danger the territory would be separated from Mexico. The Californians wanted to rule themselves. More revolutions were to follow.

Another took place in Los Angeles in 1835, when fifty newcomers from

SAN GABRIEL MISSION by Edward Vischer after Wm. Hahn, 1878, Bancroft Library; here "the music was conducted by the Indians which consisted of drums, flutes and violins—making a noise more to be compared to a riotous set of musicians than what it was intended for."
—A. Robinson

Sonora seized a cannon and with it the town. This little revolt failed. But in that year, Carlos Carrillo was deputy from Upper California to the Congress in Mexico. There he obtained an order from the president: "The pueblo of Los Angeles will become a City and the capital of the territory." In Monterey, the capital for over seventy years, this change was not accepted. Lieutenant Colonel Nicolás Gutiérrez had become governor in May and did try to establish the capital in Los Angeles according to the decree. But as he could find no one willing to donate a building for the purpose, the matter was dropped— for a while. Soon it would become a fighting issue. In this year, also, a famous crime took place near Los Angeles. Domingo Felix's wife, María del Rosario Villa, had run away with Gervasio Alipa, a vaquero from the Alamitos ranch. Felix, a grand ranchero, in time took his wife home. But while out riding one day soon after, Felix was stabbed by Alipa, while María cheered. The loving

WILD HORSES IN THE SAN FERNANDO VALLEY by James Walker, Gilcrease Institute, Tulsa
Pedro Carrillo had many horses, and he told an English friend that some of them were colored green.

couple then hid the body. Felix's empty horse and sorrowful dog told the story, and the dead Felix was found. María and her vaquero were arrested, and the angry vigilante Angeleños broke into the jail and quickly sent them to join the angels.

During this time, the breeding of cattle had increased so much that little profit was obtained from it, and none from horses, so many mares with their colts were slaughtered. Many others managed to flee, joining others so that the countryside was full of them, living wild with no owners. Their great number caused a problem for travelers, because the horses ran in groups of six or more and if a riding horse saw the wild ones it would try to join them. And if such a horse managed to do so, it was lost. The Californian who wanted good horses had only to tame them, and the wild ones were generally excellent. And even the best ones bought from an owner cost little.

The Englishman wanted to buy such a curiosity, to show at home. He came to the Carrillo ranch and said, "But these are not green." "Try to mount one," said Pedro, "and you will find him green enough."

Just as Victoria had predicted, the Californians felt neglected by Mexico, and many wanted separation. In 1836, young Juan Bautista Alvarado, with a company of American riflemen and encouraged by American ships, seized Monterey from Gutiérrez and declared Alta California a Free and Sovereign State, conditionally—until the Mother Country returned to the federal system, of which he approved. The Angeleños didn't like this. Feelings were already seething between *arribeños*, Northern Californians, and *abajeños*, Southern Californians. Alvarado, the "lion of the north," marched south to force the southerners to join his plan. The Army of the Free and Sovereign State of Alta California grew to eighty men plus twenty-five *rifleros* under Captain Graham, who "was worth twenty men, he was thought so bloodthirsty." Most important, Alvarado had a good band of music. He said music was the way to win the Angeleños. He also had a flag with a blood-red Lone Star, with the implications of the Texas story. "We see the star gleaming which will guide us to our prosperity," said Alvarado.

A California *Lone Star* flag from this period is preserved today in the Southwest Museum. Alvarado also had a flag made from the Mexican ensign, with *Independencia de México* lettered in the center field.

On to Los Angeles went Alvarado. In the city Alcalde Sepúlveda raised an Angeleño army of 270. Reaching Encino, Alvarado sent word to Rocha, who headed the angel army at San Fernando, that if they didn't give up the mission, they would all be shot. Alvarado marched there in battle formation and sent a cannon shot to where Rocha was staying—in the priest's house. Before the smoke cleared, Rocha and his nearly 300 men had decamped by the Verdugo Ranch road for Los Angeles. As Pío Pico didn't appear with help from San Diego, Los Angeles was given up. Soon after, though, Mexico promoted erring Alta California to a Department, so Alvarado returned it to Mexico and ended the conflict. "What country has so many blessings as ours?" he asked.

CALIFORNIA HORSES by James Walker, Gilcrease Institute, Tulsa; the first job in a California revolution was to collect horses. Sepúlveda provided over 100 to ride against the northerners. Each rider had a *reata* or lasso, and "there was grotesque swinging of the terrifying *reata*" in all of those revolutions. "The handling of the lasso is as important a part of their education as reading and writing are with us. Rarely need a Californian throw a second time." —Edward Vischer

Next page: a banner honoring the pueblo and its patroness, made somewhat late as shown by the remodelled church. The Porciúncula River was also called the San Gabriel River after 1825, and the Los Angeles River after 1861. The town was also called *El Pueblo de Nuestra Señora de los Angeles*, *Santa María de los Angeles*, and Padre Serra called it simply *La Porciúncula*.

NUESTRA

EL PUEBLO DE

TRANSIERUNT

GAUDIUM ERIT

CORAM ANGELIS

Et tunc mittet
angelos suos,
et congregabit
electos suos
a quattuor

uentis, a summo
terrae usque
ad summum
caeli.

Marcum 13

VETERA

DEL ESTADO   LIBRO DE

LOS AN

SEÑORA
LA REINA DE
ECCA FACTA
SUNT NOUA
DEL RIO DE
PORCIÚNCULA
INDEPENDENCIA
DE
CALIFORNIA
GELES
LA ALTA CALIFORNIA

Later, in 1836, Carlos Carrillo, who had supported Alvarado, decided that he was to be the governor. He collected an army of 100 or so full of Angeleños and marched towards the city from San Diego. Alvarado's army came down from Los Angeles and met Carrillo's at Las Flores, near San Juan Capistrano. There the dashing Captain Salvador Vallejo of the northern army flew a big flag which said IF THE ENEMY DO NOT SURRENDER I WILL HAVE THEM BEHEADED! Fortunately, they did, and he didn't. But Carrillo cried.

In 1842, Commodore Jones, U.S.N., supposing the United States and Mexico to be at war, captured Monterey. But the next day he learned that there was no war, so he gave Monterey back and sent his fine band of German musicians ashore to brighten the inhabitants' evening hours, for the Commodore was "a lover of music." "I regret the loss to the United States of the beautiful women of California," said Jones as he returned the country. He then sailed to San Pedro to apologize to the new governor, Micheltorena, in Los Angeles ("the Eden of the earth," Jones called it). The governor demanded a full set of musical instruments as reparation. Although Mr. Jones couldn't spare his, this was not the silly request the Americans thought it. For good music had

won, and would again win, the Californians over more easily than guns. Micheltorena had brought with him a battalion recruited from the prisons of Mexico, to control the Californians. These knaves made life difficult for the Californians and caused the governor to become quite unpopular. And with this excuse, in time, as usual, the Californians revolted again against the ruler from Mexico.

More and more row-loving American trappers, with their deadly long rifles, were stalking into California over the mountains, and a growing number of wide-awake American skippers were arriving by sea. They were accused of taking advantage of Mexico's neglect of the department by joining in the revolutions and hoping they might lead to an American California. When the revolt against Micheltorena broke out, Americans were found on both sides. Those from the Sacramento River, under Sutter, marched in defense of Micheltorena, for they hoped to be given some nice ranchos for their efforts.

Los Angeles, the north side, after the sketch by
Wm. Hutton, 1847, in the Huntington Library

Boastful Sutter said he would give the governor Alvarado's head on a bayonet, but instead he was captured. Los Angeles was seized for Micheltorena by J.A. Carrillo and Andrés Pico. Alvarado and José Castro resolved to take the city from them, before they could plan for its defense. Castro sent for Joaquín de la Torre and fifty-six well-mounted and well-armed volunteers, and said, "Ride at top speed to Los Angeles and take the city, if you have to kill half the population to do it." Alvarado and Castro followed them into town, and Andrés Pico was captured. Castro threatened to have Pico shot, but Pico said, "Don José, lose no time in having your sentence carried out. I come from a race that does not fear death." Alvarado persuaded Castro not to carry out his threat, and so, with handshakes, Pico went home. J.A. Carrillo was then offered the position of major general and leader of the Californians, for Alvarado said the post should go to a southerner. Alvarado was an expert diplomat and wanted to bring the *abajeños* over to his side. "Boys, I am with you," said Carrillo to the offer, and with that there were a hundred VIVAs. Pío Pico was made governor

by the Californians; Los Angeles was now all for ousting Micheltorena, too.

Captain Graham was with Micheltorena this time, and his walking infantry company looked as if it would attack the mounted Californians. But instead, Graham set up his big culvern gun, carried in an ox cart, and began to fire. Captain McKinley, with Alvarado's army, rode up to Graham and "shook hands all around. Said one to the other, 'What in the name of the great grizzly brought you here to fight us?' The united gringos withdrew to a sylvan retreat and resolved themselves into an old-fashioned picnic, agreeing to let the Californians and the Mexicans fight it out among themselves" at Cahuenga.

The next day the battle moved back through the Cahuenga Pass and into the Felix ranch, on the Los Angeles River. Pío Pico, during a dull period, summoned

Roping Cattle, San Fernando Valley
by James Walker, Dentzel Collection

Alvarado in an angry way, and said, "Bring me Micheltorena." Alvarado, the real leader, then ordered his three cannon to fire. Five minutes later Micheltorena raised up a white flag. He and his bad soldiers surrendered, marched to San Pedro, and sailed away on the bark *Don Quixote*, which flew the flag of the King of Hawaii and was sailed by Captain Hinkley. The *Don Quixote* had a band of excellent Hawaiian musicians who preceded their captain ashore whenever he had any business. The trip on the *Don Quixote* must not have

In the town of the Angels..."the houses have flat roofs, covered with bituminous pitch, brought from a place (La Brea tar pits) within four miles of the town, where this article boils up from the earth. As the liquid rises, hollow bubbles like a shell of large size are formed. When they burst, the noise is heard distinctly in the town. The material is obtained by breaking off portions that have become hard with an axe or something of the kind. The large pieces thus separated are laid on the roof, previously covered with earth, through which the pitch cannot penetrate, which is rendered liquid again by the sun..."
—James O. Pattie, 1830

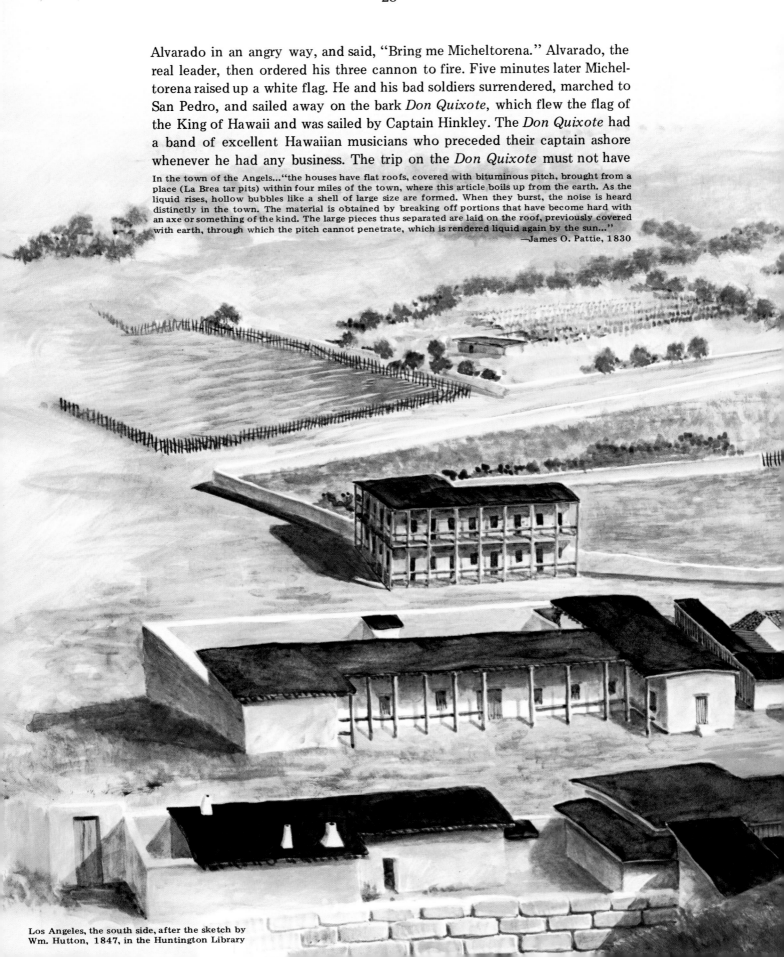

Los Angeles, the south side, after the sketch by
Wm. Hutton, 1847, in the Huntington Library

been unpleasant to General Micheltorena, nor was his leaving to the Californians. "The departure. . . of the *Don Quixote* and its cargo from California waters left the Californians in full charge of arranging the affairs of their native country as they pleased, for no one any longer had fear of an armed invasion from Mexico, which seemed to care little about preserving this frontier," said Alvarado.

"The roofs covered with tar in the heat of the day would drip down like water; and if a man or horse was caught in it after dark, when it got cool, he would need an axe to cut him out."—Wm. Russell, 1847

"The pueblo of Los Angeles is extremely rich, for the spoils from the neighboring missions have fallen into the hands of the local inhabitants; local residents own over 80,000 cattle, 25,000 horses, and 10,000 sheep. Vineyards yield 600 barrels of wine, and an equal amount of brandy."—Duflot de Mofras, 1844

José Sepúlveda, "with eyes like a sparrowhawk's," was both *alcalde* and *regidor* of Los Angeles at times during the revolutionary period. He opposed, then supported, Alvarado. In 1842 he received one of the greatest ranchos in what is today Orange County. A famous horserace took place between Sepúlveda's *Black Swan* and Pío Pico's *Sarco* at San Juan Capistrano. The stakes were 2,000 head of cattle, 1,000 horses, a rancho of four leagues (thousands of acres), plus the horses raced. The San Diegans bet huge sums on Pico and the Angeleños on Sepúlveda; the latter won, to the pueblo's joy, and he paid for the dance that night.

With Pío Pico the civil governor, Los Angeles was again the capital—except that José Castro was the military chief, with his headquarters and the customs house (i.e. the money) in the North. Pico and Castro soon hated each other, for one wily Castillero intrigued to keep them from being united. According to Osío, a prominent Californian, he followed the Central Government in believing that, if they did unite, they might easily give the department to another country. Pico schemed with British agents: California would declare its independence and then ask for British protection. But Castro was about to march on Pico, it was thought, and preparing to fight him came first.

Other Californians favored annexation to the United States. "But," said Pico, "shall we consent that the northern republic bring to our soil the horrible slavery permitted in its States?" And in Washington City, Secretary of State Buchanan felt the same way: "Further south than Monterey we should not take or hold," he said, wanting to avoid any new southern territory. But, said President Polk, "We must obtain Upper California," all of it. Back in California, José Castro made his hearers burst out laughing: "The Americans are so clever, that some day they will reach the very sky, and once there, they will change the face of the whole universe," he remarked. Slavery's days in the United States were numbered, and it never came to California. But Los Angeles was solidly secessionist during the Civil War, and Secretary Buchanan's concerns were good ones; so were Pico's.

Pico and Castro were about to make war on each other. Pico collected a force in Los Angeles to march on Castro, but other events were taking place then, too. Texas was annexed to the United States, and Mexico was going to war. Captain John C. Frémont of the U.S. Topographical Engineers was, just

A CALIFORNIA LANCER in the uniform of the *Milicia Auxiliar de Defensores de la Patria y Departamento de Californias*, by Wm. Meyers, 1846, Roosevelt Library, Hyde Park
Opposite:
José Sepúlveda by Henri Pénélon, Bowers Museum

32

by chance, leading an exploring party in the California portion of the world. A Lieutenant Archibald Gillespie of the U.S. Marine Corps arrived in Monterey and set off at a great rush to find Frémont, who was then on the way to Oregon. Gillespie, with orders for Frémont from President Polk, brought the explorers back to the Sacramento Valley. The Americans there rallied around them, and suddenly Sonoma was captured by the Bear Flag men. On July 7, 1846, Monterey was seized by Commodore Sloat, U.S.N., and Alta California was thereafter (except for a little while in the lower country) a part of the United States of America. "A great increase in the value of real estate may be anticipated," said Commodore Sloat.

ARCH. GILLESPIE MARCHING TO SAN PEDRO, p. 34
"The conquest of California did not bother the Californians, least of all the women."
—Señora Jimeno

By Lt. Col. Charles Waterhouse, USMCR

Pico, at that moment on his way north to fight Castro, met his enemy, re-treating, at Santa Marguerita near San Luis Obispo; they now had other things to do than fight each other. They reconciled and rode together to Los Angeles, which still flew the flag of Mexico. Commodore Robert ("Fighting Bob") Stockton replaced Sloat and took over the U.S. forces in California on both land and sea. Stockton landed at San Pedro with 360 Marines and sailors from the *Congress*, raised the flag, drilled his men on shore for three or four days, and then marched off at their head to capture Los Angeles, the capital of Alta California. Castro, with plenty of ammunition, cannon and horses, could have made a good fight of it, "but he wanted pluck," and cleared out. Stockton marched on over the plains—it was nearly unheard of for a frigate's crew to march—thirty miles into the enemy's country. First came the full band of music, followed by Captain Zeilen and the Marines; then Lieutenant Schenck and the web feet; then Lieutenant Tilghman and a battery of four ship's guns, mounted on four old California carts, each drawn by four big oxen. At night they camped at Temple's ranch; an alarm was given, and the loud cries of the enemy were heard, but no attack came. The men remained wide awake and under arms until finally the enemy was discovered—a couple of coyotes.

At about 4:00 in the afternoon of August 13, Lieutenant Schenck arrived at the outskirts of the town with the ship's forces; they were joined by Major Frémont with 200 men. The troops marched into town together with the band of music playing "Hail Columbia" and hoisted the Stars & Stripes in the plaza. The houses were mostly deserted, but the band did much to induce the people to return to their homes and become reconciled. A full band had never before been heard in Los Angeles, and it drew the Californians out of their hiding places. The old priest of San Gabriel, sitting by the church door, said

GENERAL ANDRÉS PICO'S HOME IN THE SAN FERNANDO MISSION
by Edward Vischer, Bancroft Library
The hero of San Pasqual had "the most pretentious adobe in the State; the building was 300 feet long, eighty feet wide, and walls four feet thick." San Fernando, founded 1797 by Lasuén, was leased to Andrés Pico in 1845.

"Ah, that music will do more service in the conquest of California than a thousand bayonets." Besides, the Commodore was passionately fond of dancing, so he gave a series of balls and fandangos for the ladies of Los Angeles.

There soon seemed to be no necessity for a large force to remain in Los Angeles, so the Commodore returned to his ship with his crew. Some of Frémont's men stayed, with Captain Gillespie in command. Gillespie had received $20,000 for expenses; rumors of an uprising to capture the money began to circulate. Gillespie now had only forty-eight men, many "perfect drunkards," whom the Californians thought they could overcome. At 3:00 A.M. on the 23rd, "it seemed as if all the devils in hell had joined in the chorus, or Gabriel had sounded his last trumpet. The Californians had a bass drum, and with its booming thought to frighten the Americans." The Americans took to the roof. In the morning 150 Californians were seen on the mesa in front of the town. Gillespie found some ancient spiked guns and had them repaired and hauled up the hill. General Flores, now commander of the Californians, soon had over 400 men and demanded Gillespie's surrender. The Americans lacked water. A thick fog told them that help wouldn't get through in time, although Juan Flores (*alias* Brown) made his famous ride of 460 miles to Monterey in fifty-two hours, only to find that the Commodore had sailed for San Francisco. Terms were accepted and the Stars & Stripes were retired from the city to San Pedro, where the Americans boarded the *Vandalia* and waited offshore. On the 6th, the frigate *Savannah* appeared with Captain Mervine, who intended to march upon Los Angeles forthwith. On the 7th, 299 Marines, sailors, &c., left for Los Angeles. As they neared Palos Verdes, the enemy appeared and opened fire. On marched Mervine, the enemy firing into his body of men. They arrived at the Domínguez ranch about 2:00 P.M. and camped there that night. October 8 found the Californians blocking the road as the Americans started off towards the capital. The Californians opened fire and caused dreadful havoc among the Marines and Sailors. The Americans formed into a solid square and charged. The Californians retired, shooting as they went. For a moment they lost their only gun, but brave Ignacio Aguilar rescued it, and they fired again and again. Captain Mervine ordered a retreat to San Pedro, and before dark the men were

Gillespie bothered the Californians with regulations: "No Californian should gallup his horse through the streets: penalty—guard house; four men should not stand talking in the street: penalty—guard house. Men caught gambling were to forfeit the money, and guard house. He broke up their fandangos, too. By such little annoyances he gained the ill-will of the inhabitants, and in order to show their respect for him, the *señoritas* sent him a present of peaches. Before sending them, however, they first rolled them in the fine fur-like prickles of the cactus fruit, and it was a full week before he got them all out of his mouth."

back aboard ship, where they remained until Commodore Stockton arrived. It had been "one of the most disgraceful defeats our arms have ever sustained," wrote Gillespie. It was Captain Mervine's fault for not taking along artillery, he added. The whipped Sailors and Marines of the *Savannah*—they had considered themselves "regular fire-eaters," now returned to the fleet with long faces.

On October 25th, Commodore Stockton and the *Congress* appeared, and the men of both ships went on shore. But on the 28th they went back on board, for the California cavalry, riding round and round a hill, made Stockton think them many more than they were. Gillespie and his men sailed for San Diego; Stockton landed the crew of the *Congress* on November 18th and prepared to march on Los Angeles.

Things were nearly ready for the march on Los Angeles when word arrived from General Kearny, who had arrived at Warner's Pass from Santa Fé with 160 of the First U.S. Dragoons. Gillespie and some of his men hurried there to tell the general that Andrés Pico was in the valley of San Pasqual with about eighty men and that Kearny "should beat up their camp." It was raining very hard when Gillespie met the general, who decided to attack the enemy at once "and take away their horses." Early on December 6th, Andrés Pico and his men were sleeping, when suddenly they heard the barking of a noisy poodle dog and the clang of heavy dragoons' swords; the sleepers arose, crying:

VIVA CALIFORNIA!
Abajo los Americanos!

The rain stopped and the moon shone bright; a shout and an Indian yell announced the American charge. But many of the Dragoons were badly mounted on tired mules. Captain Moore led a charge; the Californians made a stand and Moore fell, pierced by eight lances. The Dragoons turned, but Gillespie showed up: "Rally, men, Rally, don't turn your back, face them, face them," he cried; but all to no purpose. The Californians recognized Gillespie and surrounded him. Lances came at him from everywhere; he was thrown from his saddle and

THE BATTLE OF DOMÍNGUEZ RANCHO, also known as the Battle of the Old Woman's Cannon because the cannon, shown here, had been buried in the garden of Inocencia Reyes and was dug up for this event, October 8, 1846. By Wm. Meyers, Roosevelt Library, Hyde Park; the Domínguez Ranch House is located at 18127 South Alameda, Compton.

lanced in his chest and mouth. Gillespie got up, and, gushing blood, cut his way to the rear. The Americans buried nineteen men that night. Kit Carson rode off for help.

THE GRAND ARMIES OF THE PUEBLO

Commodore Stockton was in San Diego with about 500 Marines and Sailors from the *Congress*, the *Portsmouth*, the *Cyane*, and the *Savannah* of the Pacific Fleet. General Kearny's arrival added fifty-seven battered Dragoons to the army. Artillery numbered five guns. On the 29th of December, with Kit Carson riding in advance, the band struck up a quick-step, "Life on the Ocean Wave," and off marched the army before Commodore and General, who stood and saluted side by side. On January 8th, they came to the San Gabriel River, where Flores had promised to meet them. "We have got to cross that river," said the general from on top of his mule, "and more; we have to plant our colors in the pueblo." There was the enemy, 600 or 700 men (they thought), with glistening lances and sabres. Soon the California artillery began the battle. The gallant Commodore led the Dragoons over the river. The American artillery started to set up on the wrong side of the river. Back across came Fighting Bob. The mules carrying the guns were dragged into the river, and got stuck. In went the Commodore, to drag them out. "Now men, now pull for your lives, your Commodore is here, don't desert him, don't for the love of God lose these guns." His words were fire to the men, and with a cheer, over they went, while the Californians' shot fell all around them.

When the guns had crossed, the Commodore took charge of them himself. He was a famous gunner, and soon the Californian gun was put out of action. The General's mules stopped in the middle of the river and would go no further. Kearny got off and marched on through the water at the head of the column. Down off the hill came the Californian cavalry, in one long line, red serapes, black hats, bright lances gleaming in the sun. On, on they came, and death stared the Americans in the face. "Steady, my Jacks, reserve your fire, front rank, kneel to receive cavalry." The bayonetted muskets were placed at an

CROSSING THE RIVER SAN GABRIEL
January 8, 1847, by Wm. Meyers, Hyde Park

angle of 45 degrees, with their butts firmly buried in the earth, enclosing that mass of men in a solid body of glittering steel. "Fire!" The Californian cavalry turned, but back they came again and again. But there was a wall of steel. "Now, Jacks, at them, Charge, Charge, and take the hill," said the Old Soldier. And up they went. At their head were Fighting Bob and the Old Soldier, side by side, the one mad with excitement, the other cool as a julep. The foe took one look, and away they went. Fighting Bob now roared out for his Band, who, with instruments in hand, ran up the hill. "Where is that band?" "Here, Sir," said the Captain of the Band as those gentry, puffing and blowing, appeared. "Now here," said the Commodore, "give us 'Hail Columbia,' and in your best style, too." "Fix your pipes," he added, "and give them the d—d'st blast of 'Yankee Doodle' they ever heard. We have gained the day, hill and all," he roared.

Another crack at the Californians was expected on the large plain at the foot of the hill called the mesa, by the Los Angeles River, between the army and the pueblo. The Americans had not marched far before they saw their opponents, in battle formation. The Commodore said, "I have found out that dodging is a good thing, dodging is my trade, and I am as good a dodger as any he in California. Just keep your eyes on their Big Guns, and when you see the flash, fall down where you stand, and don't rise again till you hear the ball whistle over your heads." This move astonished the enemy, who cheered lustily, but changed their tune when the Yankees got up. The Californians prepared for a Grand Charge, and down they came at full speed, yelling and shouting. The sailors, in a square, waited; then volley after volley poured into the heroic California lancers, who then retired for another chance. On, on marched the square of soldiers. The lancers tried to break the front, the sides, the rear, but they couldn't break that square. Then they tried all sides at once. "Stand firm, my lads," said the General. On they came; and then there was one last charge. Flores said to his men: "I have only one more round of artillery to make, and my last request is, that you will make a bold and determined charge as our last resort." They advanced to within fifty yards of the American line; "they could come no further, it was beyond the power of man to face that shower of bullets, and again, for the last time, they turned and fled."

Kit Carson was in all those battles; "he was the coolest of all the cool ones who was ever in a fight. Wherever the fight was the fiercest, there was Kit, in

THE BATTLE OF THE RÍO SAN GABRIEL, January 8, 1847
The site of the battle is around Washington Boulevard and Bluff
Road, Montebello.

By Lt. Col. Charles Waterhouse, USMCR

a red shirt, pipe in his mouth, removing it only to fire."

On January 10, 1847, the battalion of sea boys marched into Los Angeles. The Stars & Stripes, hoisted by the wounded Gillespie, waved, and again the band played "Life on the Ocean Wave." The hills outside the town glittered with the lances of the brave Californians, but the Yankees had now retrieved the credit of American arms, which had been taken from Captain Mervine at San Pedro and from General Kearny at San Pasqual.

The conquest of California was due to the valiant marines, said Alvarado: "Note that I say marines and not soldiers, because had it only been a question of the soldiers who came with General Kearny to California, we would not have delayed a day in giving them passports to the Elysian Fields, had they refused to surrender," he added. Englishmen and Frenchmen in California were downcast at the outcome, for they had expected without any doubt that California would have been flying the flags of *their* countries. It was a close race, but the United States had won.

In the meantime, Colonel Frémont, with the California Battalion of Mounted Volunteers, was making his famous trek down the mission trail from Monterey, "a single bugle (and a sorry one it is)" composing the band. With just that, surely, he'd not want to be the first to march into Los Angeles. He was three months coming and arrived in the vicinity in a drenching rain, "looking worse than ever could be imagined. They were so covered with grease and slush that even the rain's good effects failed in their cleanup." Andrés Pico, the hero of San Pasqual, met Frémont and said that the Californians desired peace and were willing to come under the American government. A treaty was signed between Frémont and Pico at Cahuenga on January 15. "It is ordered by me that an entire cessation of hostilities shall take place," wrote Frémont. The conquest of California was completed. "The Americans and Californians are now but one people," said General Kearny.

The adobe house where the treaty is said to have been signed is at 3919 Lankershim Boulevard, North Hollywood.

Brigham Young had raised up 500 men for the famous Mormon Battalion, to march overland from Council Bluffs, Iowa, to Santa Fé to California. Upon arriving in California, the soldiers were ordered to Los Angeles, to relieve Frémont's Battalion. The tattered soldiers, "like Falstaff's ragged company multiplied by ten," marched into Los Angeles on March 16, 1847. "We had no waving flags, but waving rags; nor brass bands, only a solitary snare drum and fife, played by a tall Vermont fifer, and a stout, rosey-cheeked English drummer; and they struck up the Star Spangled Banner as we passed the Govern-

BATTLE OF THE MESA, January 9, 1847, by Wm. Meyers, Hyde Park

ment House, and kept it up until orders were given to break ranks and stack arms. And then came a loud hurrah from all that ragged soldiery. Their long and weary march over mountain, plain and desert, of 2,200 miles, was over," wrote Alcalde Foster. Many of the men had arrived barefooted. They remained in town until they were mustered out in June, 1847.

One Colonel Jonathan Stevenson, meanwhile, had raised up a regiment of Volunteers in New York—gentleman soldiers and rapscallions—for duty in California. Many of the patriots embarked, as did their colonel, just a step ahead of their creditors. The volunteer warriors slowly made their way by sea around South America to California. Finally, in April they landed in San Francisco, and in mid-May New York Volunteers were garrisoning the City of the Angels. They were gorgeous soldiers, in lovely red, white and blue uniforms, and best of all, they had a fine, New York-trained Band of Music with them. "I think it is the best thing we brought with us," said a Volunteer. They also brought baseball to California.

The old and the new Americans quickly took to each other—especially at dances. The great belle of Los Angeles was Isadora Bandini, one of the beautiful daughters of the arch-plotter during revolutionary days. "Ah, Isadora. . ." She had a red rose in her hair, but alas; she was dancing with one of Kearny's dark-mustachioed Dragoons. Whom did she prefer? Some said the Marines, some thought the Dragoons. But a Second Lieutenant of the New York Volunteers thought it was him. The Dragoons gave him many dark looks.

But next we hear that the Second Lieutenant of New York Volunteers had "got the blues very bad in consequence of Isadora having jilted me." There were more magnificent balls in the evenings, and to them came the Señoras Flores, Carrillo, Pico and all their delightful daughters. Now the sister of the wife of General Flores was the belle of the City of the Angels. And "Ah!" Doña Arcadia Sterns; "were it not for that hateful encumbrance of a husband she has, I should never leave California," our Volunteer sighed.

Los Angeles at that time "was certainly a nice looking place. The houses

THE BATTLE OF THE MESA by Alfred Sully, 1848, Yale University Library
The site of the battle is around 4500 Downey Road, Vernon.

generally looked neat and clean, and were well whitewashed. There were three two-story adobe houses in the city. The streets were thronged throughout the entire day with splendidly mounted and richly dressed *caballeros*, most of whom wore suits of clothes that cost $500 to $1,000 (in modern money, several thousand dollars), with saddle and horse trappings that cost even more. Of one of the Lugos it was said his horse equipment cost over $2,000 (more than the real estate of all of what became Pasadena was then worth). Everybody was rich, and money was more plentiful, at the time, than in any other place of like size in the world," said Major Horace Bell. This was due to the great demand for beef cattle in the upper country; "Los Angeles was the greatest cow country in the state. But in 1851, '52 and '53, there were more desperadoes in Los Angeles than in any place on the Pacific coast, San Francisco with its great population not excepted. It was a fact, that all of the bad characters who had been driven from the mines had taken refuge in Los Angeles, for the reason that if forced to move further on, it was only a short ride to Mexican soil. The slightest misunderstandings were settled on the spot with knife or bullet. It was a common and usual query at the bar or breakfast table, 'Well, how many were killed last night?' In 1853 there were a greater number of murders in California than in all the United States besides, and a greater number in Los Angeles than in all the rest of California."

"Human life at this period was about the cheapest thing in Los Angeles," wrote a merchant. In 1857, Juan Flores and Pancho Daniel broke out of San

Quentin Prison and went to Los Angeles. On the way they raised about fifty followers—and a revolt. They rode down to San Juan Capistrano and began taking up a collection from the citizens, but one, a stout-hearted German, refused to pay. He was therefore shot. The news reached Los Angeles, and fearless Sheriff Barton took twelve men and went to deal with the gang. On the way, José Sepúlveda warned the sheriff that more men were needed, but Barton charged on anyway. He and his men fell into a trap, and all but two were killed. When the survivors returned to town, General Andrés Pico called for volunteers to go and capture the murderers, and José Sepúlveda led a little army in finding the gang's whereabouts. The bandido chiefs were caught—and escaped—and were caught again. Their trials went like this: judge and crowd met on a veranda in town. The judge asked the villain's fate. "Thereupon someone would shout: 'Hang him!' 'Gentlemen, you have heard the motion; all those in favor of hanging So-and-So will signify by saying, Aye!' And the citizens present unanimously answered, 'Aye!' The crowd then went to the adobe jail, and the prisoner was taken up Fort Hill and 'promptly dispatched.' "

The drought of the 1860s ruined the rancheros, and land prices crashed. "Prosperity seemed to have disappeared forever." Much of Andrés Pico's San Fernando Rancho was sold in 1869, the year railroads first began to run in Los Angeles. Excitement—and land prices—then soared, as a band played and a ball was held in the new train depot. The Southern Pacific Railroad, running its line down the San Joaquin Valley, agreed to run one through Los Angeles County; when this was built, the area around it developed. In 1874, 56,000 more acres of the San Fernando Rancho were sold, and house lots were offered

"This place, whether the 'Paris of California' or not, is a hot bed of sedition, and originates all the rebellions or revolutions; and the women, they say, play an influential part." —Lt. Col. P. St. George Cooke
Los Angeles after a sketch by Henry Miller, 1856, in the Bancroft Library

El Baile

ALEX F. HARMER

Copyright, 1905.

THE FANDANGO
By Charles Nahl, Crocker Art Gallery

"The difference between a ball and a fandango is that a ball is a select gathering of invited guests for dancing and general jollification and amusement, and a fandango is open and free for all. Ladies of the higher ranks of society never go to a fandango, and Dons of the upper *ton* only go in a half-way clandestine manner. A fandango of the older time was a curious agglomeration of all the elements of the population so promiscuously thrown together in this, at that time, curious, old town."—Major Bell. The fandango was also a favorite dance which involved the improvisation and singing of verses, *sequidillas;* the Californians were very poetic.

for sale. New towns popped up everywhere. In that year Senator Jones laid out Santa Monica: a fine lot on the ocean cost $300, and a railroad train took people round-trip from Los Angeles for a dollar. The beach and bathers in nice costume were becoming appreciated. The San Fernando tunnel, 6,949 feet long, built by thousands of Chinese workers, brought development even closer. In 1886, the Santa Fé Railroad appeared in Los Angeles, in cooperation with the Southern Pacific. Then the two railroads had a falling out, and due to their rate wars, round-trip tickets from the Missouri River to Los Angeles fell to a dollar. Thousands of easterners took advantage of this bargain, and many stayed. The widely-advertised splendors of climate and scenery brought many more. They fed the Great Boom of '87. Properties changed hands several times a day. Citizens went insane with speculation, and amateur land manipulation ran amuck. Burbank was laid out by a dentist of that name, where Micheltorena had his last frolic only a few years earlier. Santa Monica now truly boomed: "One of the Grandest Panoramic Views the Human Eye ever rested upon," here just 10% down. "HO FOR THE BEACH," said the ads, and so say I. *Adiós!*